thresholds

Also by Philip Radmall and published by Ginninderra Press
Earthwork
Artwork (Picaro Poets)

Philip Radmall

thresholds

Acknowledgements

Warm thanks to the editors of the following literary magazines and anthologies in which a number of these poems first appeared:

Australian Poetry Anthology, Volume 8; *Wild* (ed. Joan Fenney, Ginninderra Press); *Grieve*, Volume 6 (Hunter Writers Centre); *Mountain Secrets* (ed. Joan Fenney, Ginninderra Press); *The Blue Nib* Literary Magazine, Issue 42; *I Protest: Poems of Dissent* (ed. Stephen Matthews, Ginninderra Press); *Milestones* (ed. Stephen Matthews, Ginninderra Press)

'Artwork' first published as a chapbook in the Picaro Poets series, (Ginninderra Press, 2019)

thresholds
ISBN 978 1 76109 429 3
Copyright © text Philip Radmall 2022
Cover image: Peter Radmall

First published 2022 by
GINNINDERRA PRESS
PO Box 3461 Port Adelaide 5015
www.ginninderrapress.com.au

Contents

At the Roadside on Skye	7
Harbinger	8
The Somme	10
A Kitchen in Connecticut	12
A Bestiary Triptych	14
On Piero della Francesca's *The Flagellation of Christ*	17
Prescience	20
Always Something	22
Happenings	24
Visitant	27
Furtherance	28
Offerings	30
Mussel Men	31
The North Sea	33
Fence Down	34
Holding On	35
Looking at the Tamar	36
The Crystal Glass Basket	38
Recherché	41
Four Riddles	42
Under 14 Soccer, Pitt Park	44
The Consolation of the Ordinary	45
Descendings	46
Artwork	47
The *Montefeltro Altarpiece*	71
Uncle Frank	77
If Poetry Were Soccer	80
Eco Zoo	81
Nothing to see here	83
Sanctum (Lockdown 2020)	84

Atoms to Atoms	86
The Gift of Poetry	87
Fells	88
About the Author	90

At the Roadside on Skye

Leaving the sealed air of the driver's side and getting out
onto heath, I took the full brunt of the wind and heights
to stand braced beside a lichened milestone, its angled
granite protrusion like a piece of the earth's bone
broken through the skin. What broke through me, then,
come far from my source, taking my reckoning?
The milestone's rough confronting; its name trying out
the memory, like capstone, loadstone, grindstone, words
to break your teeth on, meanings heavy on the tongue.
The whetstone from my father's garage bench, the hard
scrape along its oblong as he honed a chisel blade
to come keen and glinting as a horizon line. The home
hearthstone under a blaze of coals where I was forged
and shaped and drawn from. And now the milestone's
weathered markings, betraying origins or further distances,
my eyes smarting to imprint; like when I took rubbings
off a windblown gravestone, half a world away;
the dates' faint inscription; another journey line
and halt. Wherever I am, I am a brief fixed point
in blustering air, trying to get a bearing, still everything
quickly heading on; as above that roadside, a small bird,
triumphing in the blasts, wheeled and circled overhead,
travelling its course in rounds, like a winged heart,
always coming back to where it started.

Harbinger

A harbinger, we called it, the final line in the slow, withdrawing
slide of wave breaks furthering out across the sand flats before
the tide turned in. We watched for it, way out from the beach,

looked hard down at each last mark of foam and salt for the great
telling of one thing come to an end that another in turn begin;
drawn to it, yet almost hoping it would never be. Lone outcasts,

we stalked the edge of the shallows that stretched away
broad and smooth towards the long edge-curve of the earth;
where nothing was except what was still, silent, wet;

where there was hardly any depth to the world; nothing but balance
and hiatus and the vast calm emptiness of the flats; a dark
slick of cover under a grey shimmer of drained light;

as if what captured us there was something primal, unearthly,
where things came to cease a while and take in. Then we were all
instinct and reaction, happy in a quick boy girl teetering dance

and hop across the yet retreating tide, its run and halt and vanishing.
Until suddenly there it was, and gone, and it all came rushing in,
rough, uncaring, each line erased by each new incoming, telling us too

to go, retrace our steps, to heel again the firm ribbed sand
blanching to the tread, pushing us slowly to a narrow hold
of remaining beach, a last dry refuge before the sea wall

where we stood looking back, heeding it all, caught uncertain
again between the want to remain and the need to head off
into our own oncomes. Unforgettable then the sense

reflected in the solemn keeping of your become-familiar face of what will always be at any turning: the brief, intimate dilemma of a moment and its omen.

The Somme

Listening to the late wind coming in, its hard
voicings through the hardly opened window
like a low, distorted echo of what once meant

more, moves and reminds me of grandad's tight-lipped
recountings, come equally distanced and difficult,
of his days at the Somme, mustered up through all his age.

How he forced them suddenly to be, eked them
through a narrow gap in long shut-down things.
I knelt at his feet, him sat in his soft chair

leant forward, as his words ran out, lived again, stumbled
across the room and fell into stillness. Rare freaks of meaning,
summoned then gone. The bloke next to him in the trench

slumping forward, his forehead shot away; another turned
to talk, both cheeks opened up, the stub of a cigar
with a perfect hole through it dropping from his mouth.

I felt a sombre closeness, his fate borne openly
but full of an awkward conscience. I wonder if that was why
he flicked the drying-up cloth at me, later, in the kitchen,

the sting of its end on the mottle of my bare calves,
its whip-crack of speed and suddenness, the ruthless,
precise aim below my school shorts, only a laugh

coming from him; another way to get back at what got to him;
the uncompromising arbitrary fall-out of everything; the random
legacies. 'Don't tease the boy,' my gran said from the sink,

her eyes full of sorry, sending him off, then turning back
to the dishes, a slight shake of her head left and right,
shutting the window sash to stop the draught coming in.

A Kitchen in Connecticut

for Carol, Susan, and Julie Sulinski

When I came to get water from the upstairs kitchen
after a long while talking war and motorcycles
and distances with the other men sat around
in a garden that grew old and hunkered into Connecticut,

I left the far-off worlds of strangers and entered a small, closed
realm of sisterhood, tongues flapping like unravelled ropes
on a homeward-speeding truck, loosed from things long held;
years of partings and dire geography now absolved

by an ancient passport photograph that one of you
held up, all three of you staring into the blanched image
like at something not yet familiar out in a wintry fog.
The look of cold appeal, the face hardly skin,

just a pale freeze of light; but the eyes sharp as flint,
the brows heavy as iron hammered out by toil
and duty, and mouth mute with still-to-be-spoken things
that if he were to speak you would see his breath

through the grey shrine of beard carrying words
of his own time and country; and the caul of black coat
and the broad fur collar, that here was nobleman
or peasant, inviting you foreknown into his world

then leaving you still to fathom where you were,
other than to be bound together around this great
unknowing, this small, precious point of reference,
a talisman leading you to where you all again

could see yourselves the same and of the same place;
as there around the table cluttered with other remnants
like an opened almanac, shoulder to shoulder in the warm
brown light from the window thrown like a shawl gentle about you.

I took water from the faucet and carried the glass
out the door and back downstairs into the innards
of the house, through the garage, past the flag and the Harley,
and out into the garden again towards the other distances.

A Bestiary Triptych

I. The Test

There isn't much you don't know or can't fathom
through the deep set of your instinctive eyes – as with
a fox's insight into a shimmer in the forest – about your god.

But when you opened that old book of ancient teachings and pressed
your nose randomly and tentatively to a page and discovered
the mould sunk into it, strong like off old bark or undergrowth,

turning up your face, did you trouble at the words like they
too had become dank and festered and demeaned?
Or think how old truths sometimes have that smell, not to deceive

but to test your cunning; that whatever age comes off them
stales on your skin and holds there, yet to trust meanings fresh still
in your eyes, which reach deeper in, summoning you again? What came

to me was the irony of the world's mutability caught hostage
in your reaffirmingly faithful face. Then should I think only
of the flesh's mire and time's decay without seeing more

to the mystery? Tell me what your nose confronts and your eyes
resolve; alert, keening, sure. Or leave me still wanting
on the edge of the woodland's darks and glimmerings.

II. Deeps and Surfaces

For all your hurtle and hurry,
the sometimes culminating impetus of you
like you are become a gathered wave against a hull

or a fast, sudden oncome of spray
off an outcrop, happily I will feed off your deeps
and surfaces, in all the forces acting,

then rest out cormorant-like on a rock whilst you
play clamorous or calm around me, an undulant sea
that habitually surges and turns and gives.

III. Sounding the Dark

Hunting the rooms and calling out your name, the word
coming back at me off the walls, I found you, a tight black shape
in the closet's dark, hunkered, slunk into yourself,

head hung forward beneath hangers and clothes. Like years ago,
dropping bundles of old newspapers off in a barn, pushing open
the door and stepping across loose straw and sweepings, I saw

a bat slatted amongst the under-thatch and raftered eaves,
part of the high darknesses, caught alone in the thin
dagger of light that suddenly pressed into its wrap of leather.

Like you, it did not stir at my entrance or encroach,
but stayed with what it found within itself.
Sometimes, even for us, there needs to be a blindness,

an offset for all the dazzle of the light; so the bat would hang
in its inner world till the night again enclosed; as you, glamoured
in gloom, would wait till your leaden eyes lightened and cleared.

We will always find our way. Behind the graceful blur of wing
are the hard workings of skin and tendon and bone;
senses sounding the dark, navigating the luminous echoes.

On Piero della Francesca's
The Flagellation of Christ

Nothing prepares you for such a stillness
of light; the fixed geometry of form and colour
and space; like you come to it with eyes
long shut that open as the bandages
are removed and see the world stopped,
held awed and incredulous with you.
Then you are left to fathom the distant faces,
the thin, parenthetic hands, the angled feet
anchored into the strict perspective leading
to the lean, solemn torso bared and bent
to receive; a fold of skin along the stomach
like a faint confirmation that, despite the hint
of umbra, it is the body still that bears
and suffers and succumbs: the obvious,
punishable flesh. Hard, though, to sense
it fully right, even given such show;
to perceive, with the physical eye, the spirit
held sure somewhere within the deft,
crafted anatomy; confront the divine
in something made so worldly and human.
Just as they attest in implication only,
those stoic actors, quietly inflicting;
and those lookers-on, unlooking, oddly
juxtaposed, an old Byzantine gesturing more
the scourging of his own fate; that the great
martyrdom to come, the vaster light of
forgiveness and reprieve born of that pale
form, is hardly implied in this tight space;
the terse, eponymous enactment almost
unconcerning us, almost unconcerned.

Lifting my head from this artwork,
the art book splayed open carefully
on my lap, sat cramped at the window of
an old rented-out caravan, a small ribbed
carapace of steel, a hold of inner clutter
hunkered in the valley across from the main
farmhouse, in the buffeting of air coming at it
through the low-sunk, agitated light, I look
out at the farmer high up on the ridge,
a dim, encroaching figure against the grey land
rendered bleak at his back. So he comes
down at dusk from the slopes, mustering
sheep to lower ground, at the mercy
of the wind all bluster and baffle around him,
then enters his dark kitchen and turns on
the light and stands raw-faced from the air's
sharp lashings, and looks back out inert
in the soothe of the gloom. 'Hard work,'
I had said to him, earlier, his body bent
to fix the fence, the gale flapping the flanks
of his coat. 'That's right.' 'Keeping sheep.'
'That's right.' His marked, steadfast face held up
abrupt to me for a moment, its ruffled
calm, my bland platitudes, a thin, wry,
unimpressed smile on his mouth like a small
diminution in the dour, recalcitrant skin.

But what can I know of any of these lives
before me – their passions, their pathos, their dooms –
other than to look and question and suppose,
when I am full only of doubts and imaginings,
and humbled here in my own detachment?
Or infer what furtherance to their final
passing of days beyond that precise,
calibrated light, this stark, intrinsic dusk?
Impossible to wholly understand our worlds
and fates, when I feel always so fallible
in my own wisdom and faith, though I share
on my skin the same rough hold of time.
I get up, look back at the book; am like
that old Byzantine, standing slightly off,
but unavoidably a part of things
magnanimous and strange: the brief certainty
of flesh; the great intangibility of the soul.

Prescience

When you bent to pick up a few last bundles
of old newspapers squared and tied into
manageable loads stacked against the barn wall,
then raised and shouldered them and stood
all kilter and balance resting them like stooks
pivoted high on a gleaner's shoulder, or bricks
angled into a builder's hoisted hod, as if
you were at once both Arcadian and earthy,
I was all awe and wonder at your deft uplift
and heft, balanced against off-set and counter,
your arms held up and hands firm on paper-edge
and string and bulk; your father's 'There you go,
girl, I've got the rest,' as you left the barn sweet
with stilled heat and grain motes, a controlled
stealth to the car, the gentle stoop and tilt
to lower and dump them into the boot.

Then we were running back full of daring
through sharp-cut stubble, the guilt and fear
of being young and alone, your body a meteor searing
against darkening sky, trailing nascent prospect
like you would burn forever; until I saw
the bruised graze purpled on your knee from when
you ran chased and fell in the school yard,
marking and defining you mortal and actual,
your raw legs white as the bean shoots
that grew in the jar on the classroom windowsill.

Finally, our bodies stiff and arms crossed over
like the dead, we rolled through the uncut grass
to make a level weave of flattened stalks
and then lay and looked up, our palms pressed
on each other's rapid hearts so I could feel
your life next to me, a store of mysteries
and teachings yet to be revealed, a first sentience
of briefly together skin, newsprint smudged
on your glistening neck, the worked-for
bed of yielded grass sanctioning our bodies' lie.

Frail and random these faint fleets of image
that come back now only in form and outline
and passing; grained with distance but full
of prescience and telling, that life would always
be a striving for equilibriums and levellings,
a sometimes teeter to be held good in tilt
and correction, or a coveted but often
makeshift ground we each prepare for ourselves;
and love always a halt and quickening
out of incidental, tenuous things, intimate
and sheer as the shirt-cloth clung to your flat chest
mottled in the heat, dazzling as the muster of midges
shimmering above our faded faces.

Always Something

There was a mattering about everything then.
Like when he was up at the rear fence working
with those loose lines of string come astray from
the bean frame that stood rigged up as high as him;
trying to tie back the bean stems to a rough knuckle
of pole so they had something to reach for and hold
to again; a slow rain off the back field coming at him,
late on, like a final worry. Better though, when he was
out there alone, forced to quell the brunt of thought,
stare out the glitches of life through the blur of dusk.
'I'm going out,' he would say, putting the unanswerable
argument of the day to rest, leaving it in the chair
in front of the window, to tend to something more
feasible with every pull and grip and tension
of string-line, working at what he could
for all that he couldn't; to fix what could be fixed.

Things turn in on themselves, like clothes
twisting in the wash, the rain gathering
in roof runnels, spiralling into the downpipe,
bird calls circling in the low, lingering light;
like he would sit in that chair all day, thinking
about himself; how if he stepped out too far
he might come back altered, confused, unable
to re-anchor, so that it was hard to move
sometimes, caught in some strict exactness.
As if wanting to counter and shore up against
what he might otherwise find or stumble on,
all the greater inadequacies and hinderings.

Saturday nights he would pinch a bowl
between his knees, slice up the new beans
with a deft draw of the knife back towards his thumb,
watching each angled sliver's soft, absolving
plummet, then leave them to rest in water, readied
for the next day, prepared against whatever might worsen.

Maybe that is what she meant when she said,
'There's always something', watching him from
the kitchen window struggling still at those poles;
looking up the garden at him like it was all
their years, hands bound to the washing-up,
bearing her own sense of nothing ever
being fully right, and trying to hold to anything
that didn't distance more. I stood with her too,
looked at him out there in the steady drizzle,
his capped head brazening the cold, heavy-coated
and collar up, fussing with the string-lines,
scrupulous, hunkered, adamant; the young
beans hanging all wavering in the greyness,
unready, vulnerable, and needy, the light rain
fraying off the field and expected to come on.

Happenings

Because we could find solace in the sea
we drove out from the city and met up with
a vast stretched arc of shoreline and sweep
of sky, that we might get breadth and foresight
of ourselves, to be opener and unfamiliar
again. Then we were walking the wet, flat,
sand-crab-ridden sand ribbed out to the sea's
rolling edge, each wave crest's long, slow
Fibonacci arch and curve connecting it
to the mollusc's shell and the galaxy
coming up to us and withdrawing, our light
footfalls following for hours the beach
to its limit. A halt then at the land's jut,
the heavy outcrop and rise taking the sea's
letting, the broil and thrash and
flattening, and we came back different
on ourselves, our meaning to each other
dogging us again, requestioning if we were
ever right to be, always trying to pretend
we were. Vanishing behind the high-up
dwellings, the last of the sun stilled everything
into unreal light, low and diminishing
until the coastline became a coarse meeting
of matter and topography hard to make out,
like some papier mâché collage moulded
and sculpted in a weak attempt at depth
and reality, with the sand bruising under
my tread, and slow and moribund the forth
and back of the surf; and you, as if we were
each alone now, lost progressively ahead.

After the beach, how much of what was left
is still bewilderment, as when you happened
upon someone you once knew, coming back
up the hill, in the narrow street between
the houses, in the grains of the dusk, reminding
me of your past, and all your difference
come crashing down over me again.
Was that a badly timed coincidence, then, or
a brief revealing of the pattern, a hole in the
covering, showing the fine wefts of intersection
on the underside that amaze us out of our
usual reckoning. Like when I first happened
onto you, in those tunnels burrowed through
that island, deep under surface and rock,
the long, dark, threaded passageways, a moment's
impulse and clutch, unforeseen, chanced,
everything connecting, quickening in us,
the drawing ourselves in, and emerging out into
sudden newness. Remember that? 'I do,' you say,
'But I don't know what tunnel we're in now.'
One much different, then, uncertain, narrowing,
with nothing showing the way out; somewhere
in another rough, modelled relief that still tries
to recapture or replicate out of that first idea
of ourselves. Impossible to know if a thing
is right, or complete, or salvageable, like in
any art, without some small forward gleam
of faith. Otherwise, I bequeath it all
to the close and disappearance of the light.

How many times does something not happen?
Or things not come together? Perhaps the best
coincidences are those that don't happen,
that we pass on by oblivious and for no matter.
Inside the car's darkness, we looked out at nothing,
self-enclosed, unaccomplished; somehow together.
As the ignition fired, the headlamps burned
a soft foreshortened hole off-centre in the night;
then we drove off down the black road, homeward,
trusting the weak skewed bore of light ahead.

Visitant

West Belfast on a Friday night, darkness and boarded-up
shop fronts; slow, on-coming, predatory lights passing
thankfully on; his hands light on the wheel letting the car
feel a way up the Falls Road, the trespass line I'd crossed;
militant martyrs on end-of-terrace walls; his Irish drawl
thick, harsh as the engine's idle as we pulled up to a pub:
'Don't speak. Don't even open your mouth. Even your
breath has an accent. Nothing English in here.' I stood
amongst others, tight-woven as Irish knit, the shamrocked
drink-spilled carpet sticky as blood; a quiet visitant under
pictures of Provisionals, the Virgin, the naked Saviour.
By a rock face in Kakadu I stood under a 4,000-year-old
image of the creation, an earth-painted frieze of ancestors
and spirit-gods forming out the world in its Dreamtime.
Who dreamt that I too would dwell amongst these dry
rocks, these wind-blown grasses, this shallow dirt?
'All our history in this land. More'n your history here.'
Nearby, a brute, unrepentant blasting for more foothold
sinned a plundered earth that would still take us all back.
I wanted to speak out, decry, declaim. But again I felt
like a false guest, crossed over into conscience again,
with my invader's elocution, a product of my own tongue.
So I stood ground and bowed my head, silent, grateful
for land I could still put my heel down on, then trod
softly away: my pious, dissenting, but irrevocable steps.

Furtherance

for Michael Hambridge

While all the others are busy on the pebbles, dressing
and undressing awkwardly under towels, you are
the lone creature backstroking out beyond the staves

into the oncoming swell, your arms windmilling backwards
up and over and down into the sea surface, your bared upturned
torso furthering out from the land like some gradual,

indifferent leaving from us that nobody sees but me.
The last time I felt drawn to the slow wheeling of something
held in its own measure was in the quiet aftermath of fireworks

as I stayed to watch the Catherine wheel, its centre nailed
to the fence post, still spinning, receding into its core in slow,
faithful impulse, fixing me to its lasting and bringing me back to myself,

to a sweet unmattering almost of what next, stood amongst
scarves and coats and bobble-hats in air thick with darkness
and intimacy and breath, the whole brief sense of it gone

as soon as we went inside. Here then, your ineluctable
distancing stays separate and immune, that I wonder whether
you will ever turn back but remain something unlike you –

your effulgent coming-on, always broaching, always
bringing forth. Like when I sat with you at the garden table
as you scavenged from our old ground, like a bird foraging soil,

hauling up hunks of thought, unearthed findings, new tellings
of all our shambled lives as you talked fast and headlong
and I listened. But now you are a muted mark of flesh afloat

and adrift, lost in itself, sustained in a stay of solemnity and peace
and articulate rhythm far from what I thought to know, but which
now becomes you too; a gentle, consoling motion away,

looking upwards, seeing yourself in the sky, as your arms
wheel over and over, true and trusting
behind your head, and never a forwarding glance.

Offerings

for Carol

Often at night we walk together talking of ourselves,
sounding out our previous lives again against the long, soft,
subtle ruminations of traffic somewhere further off.

Up ahead, the distant splay of street lamps imaged onto the surface
of the bay's black water, where the lower rows of lights from the bridge
cleat out also upon the dark beneath, wavering separately there, all cast

like frail fragments of the hard-lit night in broken aspects
of the whole: light and echoed light, proof and sign, anchored
in strict apposition. We are all ears and eyes in these darknesses,

compelled towards the stranded offerings from antecedent things.
And you, bright lover, never dimmed nor seen but as you are,
dazzling in your bold and stark immediacy that gives hold to

what you were before me – life ineluctable, always coming back to mind –
bring me the sundered, random forms of your own reflections
scattered in your words so I can grasp them shimmering in the air.

Mussel Men

On the edge of the moor at the end of day,
facing an unknown army of days ahead,
we hold ground beside the cart on the height
of the heath, a few men now come to the cliff's
rough brink, where the arcing gulls taunt the wind
and the soft waves tease the rocks on the shingle-
sucked shore below. Then we go down to the sea,
as we do each evening on an out tide, proud
of our station, our lineage, the long heritage
of this coast. Leaning up against the cart,
we remove our sandals, peel the socks from
our white feet, roll up our flannels and stalk out
through the rocks and sea shallows, the sea sharp
about our ankles and toes. We come with nets
to collect the exposed cache of mussels, hang
the nets from the groynes, take knives and shuck
the mussels from the groyne struts and the rocks,
dig them out from the seaweed slime, working
against their grip with our angled blades,
the strength of all our years in our hands.

One by one we throw the mussels into the nets
till the nets are towers of wet, black carapace,
the prize for our craft and our purpose and our bond,
then shoulder their hold and trudge them
back to the cart and heave them on.
At last we put back on our socks and our sandals,
roll down our flannels – the rolls heavy with wet –
and pull away the cart across the shifting shingle.

Winding the cart up the cliff path, we stop
at the edge of the moor again and look
back down at the sea silent now behind us,
chock full of mussels which we'll never get,
and which we will; then turn and move on
knowing that the years too foreshorten with age
like the moor in the dusk's dull shimmer.

The North Sea

Scheveningen Beach 1982

As I stepped out into that cold, incoming sea
and let it calmly wash my feet, as if of guilt,
and bathe them in its purging surf, I watched
my skimmed stone dip and rise agnostically
across the surface, before I drew back up the beach
looking for more to cast; their inert,
unpresupposing shapes half bedded in the sand.
'What's a few miles of sea between us, anyway,'
she said, gathering up her own small stones
to take as keepsakes. Then I landed the flattest that day,
pulled it from the grey contorting tide, and skimmed it
all of twenty, thirty yards across that would-be
separating sea; as if it lasted with her faithful words,
and for a moment appeased, assuaged, believed.

Fence Down

Having been out there for hours, the fence down again,
he came slowly back in from the garden, the wind
buffeting him, his sparse hair taking flight; then the slam
of the door, the flap of coat and the uneasy settle
to the hushed atonement of the kitchen. 'I'll have to go back out.
I'm too stiff for now.' A ghost, haunting me with his last
authority, his grey, watery gaze, distant still, fathoming
what's left to it; a scoured crow foraging amongst pickings.

'Don't marry that boy, he's too wild,' said my mother's
mother. 'Like being out in a rough wind.' How he would
flirt with all the girls in the air-raid shelter, dare the bombers
defy him; lean cockily smoking up against the hay bales
tempting the lit end to the stalks; steal out on a cold night
to swap around all the neighbours' underwear
hung up on their lines for the next day; brick up
their front doors; risk, make game of; like the world
gave cause to be teased out, mixed up, disturbed.
Now it was the weather slapped back at him,
blowing down fences, pressing the world's own
irregularity through things; all got too serious to be
played up to now, toyed with. I could feel the trouble
that had grown into his heart, the worn-down tautness
of his face, the long thinking of things being never how
they should be; difficult even to keep equal with what is
when what is, is always hurrying at you too. Like it came
blustering up the path then, stiffening the slack
of the empty clotheslines, as I watched him again holding
ground at the top of the garden with the few last birds,
the broken laps of fencing askew as life, and as hard to put back.

Holding On

In memoriam Jackie Ellen Radmall

That boy up on the school stage playing bass
is ours, plying the vital art of rhythm,
crawling his left hand up and down the frets,
those cleats to step the spirit on, before holding
one note an instant longer, keeping it there
as the whole main of sound moves on.

Somewhere that note is still as it was,
but not here as it was, amongst all
of the time passed. But it helps if
a moment is more than memory, left
as it is beyond the death of its making,
something staying with its cause.

Sometimes a piece of time anchors in,
whilst the rest of time slips away besides;
hitches itself to us, and allows that time to be
for all time. Down between the chairs,
our hands held on to each other, squeezed
each other pale, hold on still.

Looking at the Tamar

Haunting the dawn amongst a ragged stook
of bankside rushes, two black swans bob and yaw
on the long, undulating phalanx of a wake
that moves away mournfully under them,
their bodies facing and turning, parting
and pairing, like things remembered and lost
and remembered again. Rising behind the back
of the hills the light holds everything up
to scrutiny and conscience again, for its right
to be, even the river checking itself, dragging
against its grainy heading, before stretching out
its brown breadth between the far-banked
tiers of tired-looking houses still in shadow
and the loop path startled with early walkers.

I could easily watch all this till the dark
gives lie to it once more, takes back the prospect
from this roused assemblage that now
confronts me with the onus to make
something of it, as if each day should be
another store of doing, to partake
with all that is and does; no point
in only having vantage. But what else
might I do with this day's slow creep of purpose,
when I am sometimes just a response,
content to gaze on already initiated things?

Even the distant estuary where the sun,
a sweating silversmith, hammers the swell
into smooth, glimmering metal, trades its gleam
to my passive eye, that curious apprentice
gently studying out how the world works.
Let me have time with this river while it
busies itself; until it darkens and the stooped
hills lean into it again like old men bowing
in dishevelled line to its passing; until
the swans, who know the harry of each
day's current, come huddling and settling
together against the late glow of boat lights,
even then keeping me up still, the on-going
nodding of recumbent hulls at anchor on the flow.

The Crystal Glass Basket

I took it across hemispheres, its awkward
glass frailty smothered in paper wrapping,
before I bared it from that covering like
a secret that even when known
still confused. I laid it on the floor,
stared it down through the stern-toned
recall of my father's voice: 'Let this
crystal glass basket pass to you now,
as it was passed to me. Take it with all
you know of permanence and change,
keep it from harm and then too pass it on,'
before he handed it me, fingering it,
thumbing off the soft clung years
like he had just unearthed it and was
gently shucking off mud and residue,
this relic hauled in fearful fealty
across centuries, myself witness now
to its preservation, like it was
nothing of itself, but of all else
unpreserved, and only it to tell.

With me it is captive, supplicant, set
deep in the cabinet, glass behind glass,
like a glint in an old crone's filmy eye, knowing
but obscure, lost in fecund meaning;
its weave of clefts and jags and prisms,
its base spinal, its sides ovalled out
into a shallow, empty hull
that it ought to float off with its
store of air but for the clear-arced
span to carry it, a slight distortion
in its line like a warp through water.

So am I host and harbourer, receiver
and guard; thrall to the laws of onus
and burden and charge; to the sudden,
nervous heart-stir of catching it in the eye;
the dread augur at the thought of it,
a laden, precarious innocence
that I dare not bring out to the world
for the guilt of something bad
happening. Except for that day I had
to move it, brought it a mute recluse
from its cowering; scooped it, careful,
slow, from the depth of the cupboard,
a weak but treacherous animal goaded
from its hollow; set it thick-swaddled
quickly into the keep of a case, away
again from our life of peril and doom.

I am sorry for him who served it to me;
its weight a tethering, its form a bondage;
a thing of no fulfilment, only bearing;
until his words and extended arms
full of release and relinquishment
worked it to me with a few last preachings
passed for me to carry away too:
'Never compromise. Always follow
your calling. Because I did, and didn't.
Do with your life what I could never do.
Be what I could not be.'

I listened; took home the basket like it was
itself a teaching: that I should bear
my own inheritances; those becomings
out of another's hopes and voicings;
that I also am a possessing onto which
new and old things hold, of strange
and unknown lasting. And so I watch it now,
shelved in its half-hidden quiet amongst
books and dust and other keepings;
then dare myself look to a farther foreseeing
when it lies ruined, smashed, scattered
into smithereens, a brute inevitability
in a rightfulness of time; suddenly a loss
but still no less a thing; unmanifested,
like a grateful sea broken on the shore,
the sense of it still whole, only its end
a different form; a vindication, all release
and peacefulness and essence; as from
a shattered body the soul at last emerges.

Recherché

I peg my favourite image of you up
to dry in the dark room of my memory,
between the first one I have of you
at that party in Greek Street,
demure and alluring, looking at me
from the far side of the room;
and that other one, much later,
of you saying a final goodbye
from behind the wheel of a
1982 Golf GL, melancholy red.

Still floating in the sink, taken just
a moment ago, is another that looks
to be a selfie of a middle-aged man
alone on a balcony in a canvas chair
writing a poem, vainly seeking
tranquillity in recollection.

I let go the pegs and watch you hang:
a naked form standing at the foot
of the bed, your small mouth open
as if saying something simple
and enticing, the backs of your hands
touching your neck, stretching out
your breasts and the last of languor.

I look back at the image in the sink;
wonder if it might yet develop into
something other than how everything did.

Four Riddles

1.

I am a line dividing air and air, separating
what isn't separable. I support and divide,
but never take sides; bear protest,
but never form opinion; stay sound in my footings,
weighted hard to the earth which founded me
and the only thing which, when I crumble,
will pity me and take back in my broken form.

2.

Someone forced me into this hold,
my girth tight against hard knuckle
in a calibration of flesh and feeling.
The purpose of my being here
is the faith put in me. I am a proof
that only fails when I am flung
into a corner and wished I never was.

3.

Let those who want to, look on me, though never
shall they see me as I am, only as I tell. I am
never alone, but always lonely; could bear
the whole world in me if I were to dare.
Sometimes I feel too deeply that I cannot
be myself; and sad that others see me
and wish themselves different, when I only
tell them what I think of them;
though what they are is never what they appear.

4.

I am the winged mercurial phantom
who flies through to stir up the world
or serve it gentle succour. I carry
no secrets only what is hidden
in the passing of my message
that you know me only by what
other things tell. I move through
like joy and sadness and time.
When I sing from the high tower of my heart,
my theme is the lone bell tolling.

Under 14 Soccer, Pitt Park

We stood out in the cold field, huddled
on the sideline, sunk into our coat-collars,
our faces blanched and our hands numbed,
only our breath's soft rise showing we were
alive beneath the low clouds sealing the sky,
sleet downing in the distance, a few birds flying
spectral above the trees in the farther field.
Hard to stay braced too long in that chill air.
Yet anchoring as the hurt of love, sometimes,
the cold's smothering hold, a pious pause
and resetting, separating us from the world's
momentum and hurry; a quiet humility
in ourselves again, before carrying on.
When someone out there scored a goal we didn't
even know it, despite the rise of voices and the
clapping, aware only of everything stopped,
the ball picked solemnly out from the net,
the slow footfall of boots on frozen ground
returning faithfully to the centre.

The Consolation of the Ordinary

In memoriam Geoffrey Gordon Radmall

Old man, what is the truth of your long pain?
I walk down the stark corridor to your room
out of the usual crowds and the traffic and the regular gloom
of evening, into ceiling lighting and signage, to where again
I can see what I can of you; but there is only the grim
urgent filliping of another vein, the needle mentoring
the blue back of your hand to take the solemn entering
of another's blood through your thin, stricken skin.
You are the earth tracked with ways, the deep river reeling
with reflections, the blown grass strewn with leavings;
now a silent body holding to life in a white mechanical bed
far from all that it did, or thought of doing, or said.
Nothing should be this different, or remote, or solitary.
Quietly, I walk back outside to the consolation of the ordinary.

Descendings

Your eyes, when I think of them, looking down from
the high country into the hunkered valleys, had that
hanker and focus for some sure hold on life; like when
I was ten and looked down the steep run of the street
from my box-cart as if I could have been descending Everest,
except for the neighbours carrying their shopping back home,
whom I had to steer around with all strength and grip
to keep the axle steady, hurtling perilously close, their pale,
shocked looks in my periphery. With the same bearing
towards trial and self-belief against all the forces pulling,
you would have stayed up there happy on heath and scrub,
reborn amongst the vast farnesses where you always saw
yourself, remote, but ardent again, all sense for all else gone;
everything there unmoving, the long makings of height
fixed firm into the ground set with steeps and plummets,
interlocked, like wheel and counter-wheel, the whole land
stilled and balanced against itself. What was more alone,
then, that place, or you in that place? Time slows, they say,
as you get higher, as if there are always strange workings
to the mechanisms of the world. As we descended, slowly,
our lives speeding up again, drawing on us, you looked
back up, a mountain-homing revenant, your eyes clinging
to a sense of lag, something of you time-caught
on those crag-toothed heights, and never coming down.

Artwork

I

It stood for years on your back bedroom windowsill at home
holding back the eye from the ocean of field beyond the fence:
E. H. Gombrich's *The Story of Art* in its dun-brown

dust jacket, the square-panelled montage of images
intriguing as the Tarot. A book of clues for breaking codes.
Many dark and prurient mysteries lurked then in your realm:

a rabbit's jaw-bone buried in the wardrobe's confined dark;
the first issues of Ambit magazine cut up and collaged into
glimpses of graphic nudes arranged on the dresser. Mulling

in my young blood, the difficult encryptions of life and death and sex
troubling me. I took the Gombrich back to my front box room,
stealthily, to summon its means of decipher.

II

You came back from school with a wrapping of crumpled
newspaper balled up under your arm and pressed tight
to your side like you had it in a head-lock.

You placed it down on the dining table and opened it up.
I watched as if at a birth – your slender, intricate fingers,
tendons working in the backs of your hands – until the human skull

was born from the wraps. 'We call it Lucy,' you said. 'For want
of a name. It will be a challenge for the pencil. I'll keep it in the wardrobe.'
Later came more skulls, small, delicate bone parts, a whole skeleton.

I saw you grow privy as Leonardo to what we are
from what we leave behind. Your room was where
the dead kept counsel; with foreboding now any entry back in.

III

Those first skull drawings I came across in your sketch book, turning
each leaf like a slow breath – the dark, open sockets; the juts
and fissures; the cracked, encompassing domes, dread against the page –

haunted me long after. The nothingness in those deeps
and hollows; something now silenced, emptied, unknown.
Then there were other sketches: people in cafés, bodies sat at tables

or queuing up; coats and jackets buttoned against the weather.
'A drawn line must be a phrase,' you said. 'A way of saying it.'
How an arm, then, rests along a table, or a hand

diligently stirs tea, or a face, looking out into the street,
quietly fashions thought. Personal, discrete, quickly done; lives
drawn into a moment and gone. Mute, anonymous their bones.

IV

I used to wait for the staircase's singular give and creak, the thin
cleft of light around the door jamb as I lay awake, then the click
of your bedroom door shutting, your presence countering

the empty darknesses. I would hear doors slamming from the street;
people crowding into cars, carried away into the night as if forever
like dim shades on Charon's barge. The dark hinted afterlife,

a different realm presaging. I thought of you in your room,
Cerberus guarding entry and exit; my mind harking you,
your being alone there too. Once I called out in the early hours,

hearing you trying to sneak a girl up, like a treachery, our parents
awoken, your bold attempt at quiet abashed, frustrated,
the stairs my ally, two pairs of footsteps unable to evade my scrutiny.

V

You painted in grandad's back room, your easel tall, incongruous
like a spacecraft landed in the centre, or some great stick animal.
Your first studio, a short walk from home; days when he'd still come

to the house for lunch, until the time he dropped from the chair
at the table, a collapse of jacket and limbs, his plummeting body
like a landslip, my last image of him. I'll be that one day, I thought.

But for then, you were painting me too in that room in a coat
black as coal and a red scarf tied round and cow-licked hair
high as a tongue's telling; kept for decades then rediscovered

rolled up in the attic; still young beneath a surface sullied
with age, like another presage, cracked as an early fresco,
or the food stains dried down the front of grandad's jacket.

VI

When, years after your leaving, I came in off the High Road, entering
the derelict shoe store, past the Buddhist workers converting it,
and wound my way up the stairs to your rented bedsit studio, emerging

into its low height, its small smudge of window glow, I felt myself evolve,
come raw and awed straight out of the school of Gombrich's
Late Renaissance, breathless into the room's gaunt dark

edged with hard light heady and glorified against the gloom
like Caravaggio's chiaroscuro. I had passed through to an upper level,
to a new reference for the mysteries, real now and tangible,

the room all paints and jars and brushes; matter for re-creating worlds,
the same but done differently; the sense of portent suddenly
held up to me like your arms thrust out wide in welcome.

VII

A sort of vigil the way the painter sits before his easel looking
at the windowed corner of the room, the model arched forward
on the edge of the worn, shell-backed sofa, hunched naked like a fallen Eve.

Between that scene and the canvas edge, a narrow sliver of angle
so as not to delay the eye's transit. The cuffed wrist resting
on the mahl stick. The brush tip's deft observance. 'You're good,'

others said. 'And young. Why don't you go off, travel, paint
different things instead of that old sofa all the time and those
nudes. And people want abstracts these days.' You worked on,

unbothered, faithful, unassuming. 'The best work is done without ego,'
you said. Today my heart plaits a wreath of evergreen shoots
and buds to lay around your devoted, humble, unswayable head.

VIII

When I was fourteen and first staying with you, I passed one
silk-robed on the stairs, on her way up from the bathroom
to your studio room as I was taking leave for the kitchen.

I confess, I waited a little as you readied, then slowly came
back up to the closed door, bent, and peered through
the keyhole for sight of the nude in the flesh;

my sly but tentative trespass, my heart urgent and travailing,
trying to suppress breath and guilt. But the alignment
not quite right between keyhole and sofa, my eye

still teasing the line of sight to bend as if light might transgress too.
'I feel wrong doing this one,' you said, afterwards. 'It's for her husband.'
As we sat cold by the unlit stove, suppressed in our respective sins.

IX

Tubes of paint, new and partly used, arranged in neat rows; brushes
splayed like votive tapers from dirty jars; turpentine pooled
in tin lids; a redolence of instance and awe; raw matter readied

for alchemy. You told me how Turner had himself strapped
to the mast of a ship in a storm, his body wrenched and flung
in the turbulent hail; hurled through the vortices; flashings, flailings,

the sense of it all carried back in his nerves and blood to be
lashed down onto the canvas, one with the paint's transmutation.
The artist as crazed being, I thought, as you stood anchored

to the four walls and the room, checking the light, the sofa; furtive,
meticulous; readying your own base substances to change and perfect;
my mind held mesmerised in the eye of your madness.

X

Fluffy-slippered, feather-hatted: the quirk of ridiculousness
parading the raw, sallow, pelt-like nudes, cross-legged, stiff, or sagged
against the sofa arm; self-absorbed, indifferent, distant.

I had left someone in bed, brazen, wanton, supine on pillows
like Goya's *Nude Maja*. What did I meet then long-wrought in your head?
What forlorn images come sundered from your loins? Do you recall

how our mother used to say you only wanted to paint nudes
to get them into bed? What would she have made of these
off-beat, cold-lit depictions, stark and veined and unreadied?

The romance of anatomy was what you always saw there though,
with your coveting eye: intimate forms, hard in their insouciant skin;
all their ambiguity roused in a breast's softly shadowed slump.

XI

Piero. Filippo. Greeting each other like poor apprentices
of the High Renaissance: painter and poet, brave, forsaking,
unknown, that art most glorifies where most it is humble.

I am sitting on your bed in the mess and dinge as you
pack away, in the drone of traffic from the High Road below
trying to drown us out as we talk again of our modes of doing,

of how to say things true: what is unsayable any other way;
me, grappling the hard bodies of words; you, wrestling the paint's
tough muscle; then looking at each other in the after-pause,

silent, smiling, our lives to be so much apart, but now without
distance or doubt, with the understanding that needs
no talk, nor paint, nor words. Ah Filippo. Ah Piero.

XII

Leaf matter gathered from the street and heaped upon the floor
high as a harvest bale; toy boats, cars, animals a-play on the sofa;
newspaper screwed up around like a raging sea; rough, anachronistic;

abstracted realia. Always seeing in something, something else.
Remember when the call went out about the inspection and you
pulled up all the tomato plants from the garden instead of the cannabis;

took them earth-dripping upstairs and hid them in the wardrobe;
a dark abundance of nightshade leaves, wilting in the stale air
amongst close-hung neglected clothes. Slowly they were

transplanted back, snug again in their plot beside the innocent weed;
only later for their fruits to be more intently reclaimed, redeemed, transmuted;
a still life of them all ranged out on the sill like a pall of setting suns.

XIII

The room felt like a murder scene of paint after he had done
his work there. From outside, on the stairs, coming to it slowly,
you could already smell the paint on the air; a first telling,

still needing to be made sense of; the itch of it
in the nose, the eyes; the faint touch on the skin like it had
breath. Then, in the room, the blatant evidence:

the pallet's mess, a massacre of colour and slaughtered matter;
paint on the brushes and table and on his clothes; paint spattered
over everything like a spent, molested force, but still warm,

accusing at the last. 'Look at what has happened here,'
it said. 'Look at what he has done to me. And there,' –
pointing to the easel, the canvas – 'there is your motive!'

XIV

The floorboards groaning like the deck of a lurching ship,
one hunched being pacing at the helm; the window crack letting in
a dying breath of exhausted air from the street where others render

scattered thoughts and litter baulks up the entries. Fledgling tubes
resting like settled birds on the table spread with newspaper
like a landscape where every field tells a story. Books, open

and provocative on the bed, and old finished canvases
hung around the walls like a foreknowing. Oils and brushes
readied in supplication for the spirit that serves time

in the prison of its ideas. And easelled up before a faithful eye
the next small gift back to a world as the lightly held brush finally
transfers to a clamorous surface and proves the mind miraculous.

XV

Was it something in your clothes confirmed you, or in your skin?
Held you in place, bore you through years of weathering:
oils, residues, tinctures, pigments, wearing at your surfaces,

infusing, scouring; each time I pressed to you again, the earthy must
of things long been the same. Like that day you stood sketching
the escarpments, bent short as Lautrec over the page in your familiar,

cerulean blue jumper that you'd often sleep and wake up in. Or when
you came bouncing down the street in the '60s, hair blown
like Van Gogh's stars, the builders wolf-whistling you.

'Get your hair cut by tonight.' 'Yes dad.' But coming back
the same, your small wilful body embarked on art, impervious,
striding lightly but never more certain upon the pavement.

XVI

Muted, dazzling, these portraits, done for money, like this one:
how just the faintest of window light rounds the face; calm, Dutch-like,
intricate; how a pallid glint of white cornered in the eye raises it

above archetype to the personal; the attested life. I could talk of these
faces for hours, these bold likenesses, your epiphanies of vision.
You live in the symbiotic world, where paint and image

work silently off each other. But is it the image that moves me,
or the paint? The face in the picture is there for me, in the pigments,
but not really there as the pigments are. So what do I know?

The mark or the meaning? The leaves shimmering, or the sanctity?
The last bird fading into the sunset, or the lingering sadness?
Who can say what is? Only the light, which perceives all.

XVII

If you look enough at this creature of paint, the large head,
grey-fleshed and skull-capped, voluminously bearded, this show
of scrupulous capture, to see into the life instilled,

its being and purpose, think how much behind is doubt and anguish
to get to this; the difficult prevalence over all else, to make
and dare to claim the making; the signature at the bottom

in neat uncursive hand, almost a print, liable for all
apparent here. An experiment with eternity, perhaps.
But does it stay anything, or what it says stay anything?

I see so much the need and struggle to create; a living thing grafted
new to the world, but always imperfect, challenging back its maker;
the despair and retribution of fulfilment, culmination and end.

XVIII

Was it the level lie of the land all the way to the horizon
or the wind bearing westward that braced us, expectant,
lee side to the outhouse wall to watch the day coming on,

a hushed, open purpose stretched out like a newly sized canvas?
That polder country we visited, exposed, isolating, raw.
Is it in art where I should look for meanings, or in the world?

To know why things are. In your room are always new tellings;
fresh renderings; each great flash of faith; another face
inferring from the easel; eyes deep as distance swallowing sight.

There are acres sometimes between what I see and understand; often just
things that briefly startle the emptiness; like that bird you spotted,
a speck of hurry, glimpsed then lost, miles away on the wind.

XIX

Seascapes opened in you, like a foreknowing, or a hole formed
in sculptured bronze seen clearly through; called you coast-wards
to a reckoning at the edge of things; shorings; harbourings.

Suddenly you knew all about the sea's movements, tide levels, swells;
its moods and turnings. I would come see you, though less often,
your body small still in a doorway, humbly governing its realm.

I thought of Verrocchio's David, all slightness, boyishness, strength.
Inside were canvases full of the sea's dark power; thick flails
of blacks and greys and purples, great swaths of wave and trough

wielded at the harbour wall. I stood back as you removed one
from the easel, a great grimacing ocean, long shocks of paint,
and laid it down like a vanquished giant's head at your meek, soft-shod feet.

XX

Detritus, gutweed, bladderwrack, dragged up in the wave's
sleek underbelly, the sea coming in from way out.
We walked the beach below the sea wall between the steps

down, hurrying before the tide trapped us. You walked ahead,
gently, but headlong, uncompromising. 'Life is experience,'
you once said, 'but talent is responsibility,' your fierce purpose

long quickened in you, whatever else was caught up: marriage, age,
poverty, the reluctant pulling-back sometimes into practicality.
I felt a blur of spray and looked off. The sea, also, is implacable.

We were still between steps, but closer to the ones come from.
'We'll have to return to go on,' you said. Another small compromise,
glimpsed on your face like a far-off wave-break against the sea's full oncome.

XXI

Deep metaphysics over the washing up. Answers to time and existence
sought for at the kitchen window, mirroring everything back.
But where I hankered sharp truths, I saw more and more

how you lurked on the cusps; the blurred edges where things become
disturbed, unclear; Turner's light burning everything into indistinctness;
an almost oblivion. Like you would sit at your table, the sun setting

somewhere over the sea, crumble the dried weed into the tobacco,
constructing each new cigarette, light an end and suck in, your mouth-open,
head-back draw of smoke, holding it down like you would die, then

drawing even deeper. Useless then to talk; only the gulls filling the silences.
Better for me to go, return later to try for answers, you too far through
the transience, your brown eyes leaching into Turner's seething colours.

XXII

What else burned fiercely in you and held you alive?
Goya's dark visions as much as Turner's dazzle. The process of art
is a working backwards into the making. One day I would see

a work completed; the next, rubbed over with newspaper.
Like a boot-black, polishing and polishing a boot to a shine; then
spitting on it till it's matt again; then polishing to the final brilliance.

Creation and destruction. Reality and representation. Dying and living.
Separate, but inseparable. How easily different things can sit with each other.
As I sat beside you at the last, watching your eyelids fibrillate.

'I have dark dreams. Nightmares.' 'I'm sorry.' 'No,' you said,
'I welcome them.' Black, I thought, as if from Goya's brush; giants
dangling you up to consume you inside your vivid, ravaged mind.

XXIII

Tell me the last thing that filled your head. A gull's deep swoop
above the swells; the hushed slither of evening tide; the boats
in harbour, rocked by the wind; the shimmy of mast ropes tolling?

Or that fairground clairvoyant: 'You will live out your days by the sea.'
Did she foresee too your quick death; the sudden hurry of life from you?
I watched you lying there in that sparse room. 'At times,' you said,

'when I draw, I draw the edges of things around the object, as if the object
itself is not the thing.' And so my eye saw only the borders of things around you,
taking in the line of pillow and sheet and blanket, as if ignoring you.

Something there though had seen more than I ever will, and hearing
a late gull-call over the room, turned a small head gone almost to skull
towards the last play of the sun and passed into the blessing of the dark.

XXIV

Returning to you not there, only the same accoutrements
of the studio: the brushes in their jars; the pallet; the eyeglasses
waiting to see again; the neat arrangement of things; except

the mess of the woman hunched forlorn in a chair upstairs never wanting
to go back in there; what then was left of the questions still coursing
my blood, as I fumbled through the paintings stacked against the wall,

turned in to one another like a found peace? 'Sometimes,' you once said,
'it is best not to trouble for answers, but to leave it at the questions.' So if
I think of anything, now, it is of that last work unfinished on the easel;

something of itself uncertain, curious, only half-knowing. I imagined it
even then, standing there for years like a remnant ghost, as I closed the door
softly, and walked out to all I could only wonder on.

The *Montefeltro Altarpiece*

'If nothing else than this, then what?' you ask,
in the flush of aftermath, the warmth still
coming off you, bared and bedded and aghast,
sensing life's fate again, the doomed flesh,
turned to me in the dark like we have been
caught out in a sudden glare of being. To answer this,
I would have to go back, see myself young again,
a small gang of us heading into a tunnel arch
cut deep through an embankment carrying the railway
behind the houses; coming running and shouting,
trespassers, rough-clothed and tousled, strong
in our bluff bravery, stealing in to confront
the tunnel's darkness, to out the whole unscrupulous
truth of it lurking high in the hang of the curved
black roof all tessellated brick and seepage,
walled up from the bog sludge and the slow-flowing
bilge of a narrow watercourse moving through
from the outer world over drowned rocks and debris
and banked in by planks edge-laid against the mud
where we stood and looked up and wondered.

An intimate darkness, stored for each time
we would come; a faint light, remnant only on
edge and angle, showing the darkness more;
nocturnal beings, there to exploit the offerings
of a bleak realm, to receive ciphers and oracles,
face to face with stillness and awe; in a place
emptied of trappings, down to the raw rudiments
of the earth; a halt of quiet, except for the earie run
above of the railway's sudden, dull, intermittent drone.

We poked sticks, brought in from the outside, into
the tunnel water, for this is what you do when you are
young and alive, stir up the surface, beckon something
from it, more than the smell, or the disturbance itself,
worth the hard conscience of our dare and entrance
that whatever might come out would overwhelm
and yield up to us, reveal and proclaim, gifts
of revelation against all we thought we knew;
something beyond precedence or forethought,
of who we were and why, beings to be more easily
explained than we yet knew, that I was like a sensor
readied, alert, poised on the plank's thin edge, staring
into the black trembling space and its boundaries,
unsure if it was the darkness afraid, or me;
expectant, prone, waiting in the great grant of life.

Then, suddenly, I am in a school art room studying out
a picture of Piero della Francesca's *Montefeltro Altarpiece*;
the way those figures too stand and look away
from themselves, under an apse arch that roofs them,
but here steeped hard in light and colour, a luminous
geometry of paint; eyes enlightened, like they know
already; how they wait within; their holy passivity
against our almost astonishment at their ease of stance
and carriage, the fluted folds of garments and the smooth
plated armour. It is like they could stay forever like that,
in mute acceptance of what they are: watchers, players,
swathed in the midst of contemplation; making
manifest the mystery they are there to acknowledge:

birth and flesh as death and saviour; the child held firm
on the lap, the innocence carrying all our sin,
reminding us of our bound inheritance; doom
and redemption vying against each other, while
they hold to time in a firm calm of faith, all patience
and sanctity, damned but as yet uncondemned.

High, obdurate shouts, hollerings, howlings
into the abyss, the recalcitrance of echoes.
Then I heard a tossed stone plummet and sink into
the surface of the watercourse, bringing me back
to my dire presence, a being struck fast still
to that dark place, tethered to its rank airs and muds
and waters, staring into the firm, mirk-full ripple-spread,
reaching out, my own face broken across
its inky breach, floundering there in the heavy
mix of form and rotten substance, smirched
with the same darkness, the faint light
showing my body crouched and fallen,
rent to the outcome of that trespass;
that I had not just come wrongly there
but had come bad into the world, to bear myself
until my end for what I could not account for;
to suffer having done no wrong; something
made flesh and bone and death, a dread
felt for the sin of being, struggling to know why,
except to each night bear sacrifice and appeal,
hunkered at the bedside, alone with the soul
held in the rough bonds of skin, safe only in the
protection of prayers and pity and mute mouthings.

The next time I am back there I am up
on the field's edge, just away from the houses,
looking across to the embankment, stood long
in the daylight watching for trains, catching
the onset of a hub of sound and then the quick,
slick carriage-blur across the eye, figures in windows
flashed suddenly into being, come visible
and lost, specks hurried to different
destinations but the same end, the fury
then the silence, the stillness of the after air,
a purpose felt and gone, as I stand and stare
and wave them all away. I look for something
sure to cling to, to hold me still, fix me.
And I am off, to the place I know, to confront
the dark again, to test, alone this time, its vision,
following the route of the water, lowering,
reaching the bottom, treading in the narrow run
of the gulley, and I am up to the embankment
in through the arch's opening, sludge-splattered,
shoe-sodden, locked in the gape and draw
of it again, the tunnel's fearsome brunt;
but summoned deeper now, gone in to its hilt,
only blackness reflected back and pressing in,
as the heart harries and the feet find anchor
and I wait hot in my after-hurry. A rumble above,
slow, undulant shudders of the brick; long, low
corrugations of sound move through and away
and leave me feeling more alone, as I stand fast
on the plank's sliver of edge. This time I let

the mire and the wet come upon me, allow
the dankness in, close my eyes and give myself
to this place; that now I am just matter and substance,
something forged and wrought out of this
darkness and cold, drawn from the earth,
drips sparking innocent on my upheld face;
like I am warm ground taking rain, white-heated
iron slaked with fresh-drawn water, a lone,
raw thing, shed of legacy; for this time, freed from the caul
of wickedness and sin; wrested from the prescribed
learning of death's doom and judgement; from the
dread and fate of Piero's figures in their
solemn hurtle of days, always looking away
towards something else in the light and hope
of their unworldly detachment. For I am
safe in the body's keep, whole, bounded,
grateful for its clutch and stay, for the chill air
soothing the breath, tempering the trembling blood,
and on the skin, the soft, absolving damp; for here
in the darkness, in the flesh, can be the blessing.

So where does that leave us? Two shapes
in this blackened room; me, now, in muted
sight of you, the want pressing through the need;
you bared and allowing, the body turned all
to lust and granting, the yearn and the yield
in your tightening arms, the hands that run along,
and the fingers that seek and summon up the sense.

Let this unlearning come again, from the shadows
that linger in the rounds and hollows
of your skin, that cleave and break across your form,
so I might pause again, held dazzled in your darknesses
as in the tunnel's dread suffrage proffering
the body's own redemption: untrammelled
passengers sundered here from our fateful course
and from the guilt of being alive. If nothing else, then this.

Uncle Frank

Each time when he came to us with his stories
and took us along the old, countrified track
of his voice, all twisted vowels and hard
glottal stops, travelling its rough, unsealed
surface on journeys we would for months look
back and marvel on, the day became worthier
than it had been. I was just passing, he would say,
clenching his yellowed teeth around the straight
stem of his pipe, on his way to taking his wife,
my aunt Molly, to visit her sister, May, my grandma.
As he settled himself, all dark suit and large
knuckled hands, into the chair by the window,
he would smile knowingly and let me go out
to his sleek, black Austin 8, parked at the foot
of our slick, unused asphalt driveway,
and I'd climb in and breathe the umber brown
leather coachwork and tobacco smells and grip
the large wooden steering wheel his own large
hands would grip, and think him like some
fantastical peddler come from far off lands
to sell tales and reminiscences, where distance
was still a longing anywhere beyond the streets
and fields around, and the Austin a conveyance
you might wish yourself anywhere in. When I came
back full of wonder and longing he'd tell me
how the butterfly had wings of gold
and the firefly wings of flame, and how
the little flea had none at all but got there
just the same. I took in his jocund counsel;

his lilting cadences, his rolled, lingering r's.
Even more, his risky whimsy and his far-
fetched other-worldliness. How his great, great,
great grandfather had poked Lord Nelson's eye,
the patched one, the flesh squishy as an orange
you put your finger in; how he'd seen dinosaurs
on the Jurassic coast, and had kissed the Blarney
Stone and brought a piece of it back, and how he
and grandad had hoodwinked Molly's friend
to kiss it for the luck it would bring and had led her
blindfolded so as not to harm the spell to where
she'd kiss the soft cleft of grandad's pressed-
together forearms and the shock and laughter
on her face when she removed the blindfold
and saw him pretending to pull his trousers up.
I watched his lips pucker as he went back to sucking
and puffing, his legs crossed and head back, his long
hobnail fingers tending the pipe's bowl, holding
steady a new-lit, drawn-on match, his cheery
museful face gone way out beyond the window.

Years later, it was us visiting him, after
Molly died, when he had to live on his own
in a small serviced apartment and we stood
with him a while in the confined kitchen
with its packed-around shelves, and all
he talked about was how he could do
everything in there from the one spot, miming
the picking up and the dealing with and the
putting away of plates and bowls without
moving his feet, his pipe hands-free in the
inscrutable clench of his mouth; unconveyanced
now, unjourneying, defined only by what
was within reach. 'Good of you to stop by
on your way,' he said, seeing us off, as I
watched him from the back seat of our first
car, whatever our way was, him stood smiling
from his porch, all his dined-out-on distances
finally shelved like the close, neat stacks
of crockery arranged around his kitchen walls.

If Poetry Were Soccer

We can't get too carried away as there's still
a long way to go, so we'll just be taking it one poem
at a time. You can judge it how you want,
but, in my opinion, you're only as good
as your last poem. At the end of the day, it was
definitely a poem of two halves. That was never a poem,
anyone could see that. I think it's really unfortunate
that he had to save his worst poem till last.
He's taken a few knocks, so we'll just have to see
how he pulls up for the next poem. Poetry is not
a matter of life and death; it's far more serious than that.
That was definitely the best poem we'll see all season.
He's a poet with so much potential, it's a pity he's so
prone to injury. The problem with poets these days
is they earn far too much money. As far as I'm concerned
there's only one winner today, and that's poetry.

Eco Zoo

The Ecomuseum Zoo is a Canadian zoological park in
Sainte-Anne-de-Bellevue, Quebec. All the species are local to
Quebec and have been taken in because they could not have
survived in the wild.

I. The Owl

The owl sleeps cowled in darkness deep
in its niche of the tree. Around it stretches
the pond's green skein, rough weeds
anchoring the banks, a low tangled
undergrowth, a rich, algaed glow.
Grey in its enclave, it is sudden lumbering take-off
and silent flight all still to happen; a keep
of keen unerring sight and deft trajectory.
Think how to look on it: something that does
nothing yet; that tells of nothing yet;
an unstirring imminent navigator
of the nightscapes; an expanse of knowledge
before it is known; a vast new analogue of time
stilled before its movement. Leave, before it is
too late, and all this prospect spoiled.

II. The Wolf

The wolf stands with its lean head turned to you,
its mind roaming lush distances, measuring horizons.
But it looms there like its own landscape: the long
crag of its face, the jut and cleft and edge;
its body's soft topography like smooth untrodden heath
shimmering under the sun's height. To it, you are
at first a sense of something, a surmise. Then,
sharp as flint, its grey eyes strike from their cave
and fix you there, mark that they have seen you,
before it moves away into the shade, knowing
you are always kept behind the fence,
as you all walk on, separate, processional, safe.
How long, it thinks, before you can break from your captivity?

III. The Lynx

The lynx is there but not there.
That you cannot see it proves
it is the lynx you do not see,
even though the lynx is everywhere
and all you see is the lynx.
Benefactor of grace,
it lurks in the triangulation
of your despair and hope and belief,
mysteriously transcending your eye,
constantly challenging your faith.

Nothing to see here

When we reached at last the rough edge
of coast, and came fast upon the violent assault
of the sea on a small group of fallen rocks

lying hunched and age-marked and cowering
like they were poor, supplicant vagrants, their blotched
and algaed forms repeatedly scourged and beaten,

we became as witnesses, stumbling across
something else's cause; though the sea hardly
noticed us in its brute compulsion, except for its

every so often rising up and giving pause,
as if taken by the look of something looking.
Best give it leave, I thought. Which was why

I shuddered as you stepped out onto a far-most
ledge, facing the sea's face, willing to take it on
like you had to be the one to confront it,

friend of rocks and innocence, against my knowing
that I would have to be the one to help defend you; until
we were moved on by the shifting wind, coming up

strong beside us. 'Go now,' it said. 'Walk away,' turning us
back, like it was itself some colluder in all this. 'Surely
you have other things to do. Nothing to see here.'

Sanctum (Lockdown 2020)

When I went out in the early light to the walled brick
at the end of the garden, the first bird sounds,
each long, short, rise and fall of note, were like
a calling, summoning me down to look back at where

I live. The bent magnolia bowing its head like
a monk at prayer; hedges seeking higher station
behind the washing line's worldly apparel: shirts
hung like sufferings; diurnal rounds of underwear,

their familiar clefts and junctures and pairings;
and what was hefted out to the middle once,
the sundial's monolithic plinth; in the burgeoning light,
the gnomon's lurking shadow. And if this were

the last of days, could I feel any more estranged
from what else lies beyond these intimate borders,
the grey obsolescence of the fences; or be otherwise left
with nothing but a sense of vague abstract things,

remembrances of instances, and the words of others;
what I have been and done and wished I'd done;
things unventurable to now, or ungetbackable to,
confined to this house's stark sanctum, its dark,

encompassing brick? But I am reminded that only
the earth at my feet is certain; all else is untaken steps
or blocked paths or re-covered tracks. So I comply
with what is here, conceding to this limit of ground,

this small vicinity of sky, however the day
still tests me, where I can see the light
still working on everything, right until the close
of evening when the birds announce its leave.

Atoms to Atoms

And then suddenly you appear to me
something foreknown but still unprepared for,
come as from a distance after I have

waited, looking towards the stairs, this long time.
And all the air takes breath, holds it, and only gradually
lets it ripple back across its reach. I feel the wake

of it settle, then the quick, almost-hurt as the atoms in me
riot and rush in a strong, heart-sprung, unruly
charge to you away from their normal cause, pulled

towards your own by a greater force than keeps them;
a hurry, leaving the flesh run through. I stand and look at you;
a watchman fathoming what's in his plain of sight

with a new scrutiny towards things no longer ordinary;
as if the usual, regular come and pass has dropped
its own strict guard a moment and allowed such difference in.

Strange then to think how the whole of what we call love
can still come down to the astonishment at one thing:
the sight of you there looking back at me, a truth

swaying my instinct again to arm you whole and round;
and when the laws of physics stop me at your skin,
to break them with this anarchy from the heart.

The Gift of Poetry

How should I respond to the last show of faith
from the day's slow dusk, its tinge of suffering
as it holds up at the end some final offering;
except to feel it linger in a swathe
of swooping wings arcing above the earth's
brown fallow before the graceful fold to ground
of the flock's downing; or in the paling sun found
bedding itself away humbly into the dearth
of light at the world's edge like some vagrant,
fortune-lost, done for the day and gone blanketed
into the recess of a shopfront doorway. So I plead
the lasting tenure of such passing images rent
against the growing darkness; my mind still lit,
these few loosed sparks of words fading off the lip.

Fells

After my brother's funeral, I drive north across England
looking for crag tops and ridge lines and high scrub; for steeps
lifted out of catchments; for the juts and brunts of an old earth
set firm in its exposed face and inward thoughts. That if there is to be
a telling out of this, a lore to guide me now, it will be riddled
through some stark fell side, looming and dour and obdurate,
baulked up blunt and hard to the meek give of sky beyond.
Like I should show to it my own ground, the great shifted mass
of being brotherless, the sudden upthrust and tear through heart
and matter so I am pushed and sundered, broken away and recast
like a new world formed, bleak and alone and left with it all trying to settle.

As I step out and climb into these hills, the sense of them deepening
further from their base, they are damp with the last day's rain, bog-marked
underfoot and scored with run-off, until they steepen quickly into
open slope and moor and stand out barren and scoured, bearing visible
their years, above a valley left slunk in its vast down-width and reach,
and all around is heady with distance and awe, sheer and leaning
and unfamiliar, as I press another foot down and trust to it for all that.
Now I am high out of harm from him, from his gaunt form
sunk in the low bed which, if I caught or touched, cried out
with pain from him that crippled me to the chair where I sat watching
the inertia of each heaved breath's thin clutch and catch and groan.
Too late for talk or questions, only the set image of his slow leaving,
in the half-dark of the small room's last grasp of him, where the stiff
bone-racked body stayed and pulsed for its own sake still.

So I huddle against a boulder's anchoring on the flat gorse and the scree, on a hill face made resolute by weather, welted by winds and tested by the lengthenings and shortenings of millions of days, its ground stolid and unflinched and coping, as I watch the late mist coming and the heights of these fells closing into their own introspection, and the light softening against it all, and press to the lichen cold and wait for instruction.

About the Author

Philip Radmall is a poet, novelist and teacher. His poems have been published widely in literary magazines and anthologies in Australia and internationally, including *Overland, The Blue Nib Literary Magazine, The Australian Poetry Anthology*, and the milestone 1991 UK anthology *Grandchildren of Albion*. His novel, *Painting St. Feoc*, was published in 2003. Awards for his poetry include two third-place prizes and a commendation in the Newcastle Poetry Prize (Australia), and an editors' commendation in the 2018 Hunter Writers Centre *Grieve* anthology (Australia). His first full poetry collection, *Earthwork,* was published in 2017, and his chapbook, *Artwork,* in 2019, both by Ginninderra Press. He is a senior teacher of English language at Macquarie University in Sydney.

www.ingramcontent.com/pod-product-compliance
Lightning Source LLC
Chambersburg PA
CBHW070313120526
44590CB00017B/2662